I NEED A DRINK

KNOCK KNOCK®
LOS ANGELES, CALIFORNIA

Created, published, and distributed by Knock Knock
6080 Center Drive
Los Angeles, CA 90045
knockknockstuff.com
Knock Knock is a registered trademark of Knock Knock LLC
Inner-Truth is a registered trademark of Knock Knock LLC

ISBN: 978-168349105-7
UPC: 825703-50155-1

10 9 8 7 6 5 4 3

I NEED A DRINK.
YOU NEED A DRINK.
WE ALL NEED A DRINK.

WITH ALL THE CRUMMY STUFF GOING ON IN THE WORLD (AND OUR OWN LIVES), IT'S tempting to just blot it all out by knocking back a glass of good Malbec or downing a few Jell-O shots. War, poverty, misogyny, stupidity, trolls, unnecessary apostrophes, paper cuts: it's a wonder everyone isn't drinking alone at home in his or her underwear. (This is so tempting, the Finns have a specific word for it: *kalsarikannit*.) While having a drink is often an excellent immediate solution to your woes, it's not so great in excess or over the long-term.

Alcohol has been the quick fix to life's little and big slights longer than pretty much anything else—medication, meditation, primal screams, or kickboxing. In fact, there are anthropologists who theorize that humans first cultivated grain not for bread but for beer (i.e., the need for beer is what led to civilization). Clearly, boozing is a well-worn escape.

But it's not for everyone. So what's the alternative? There are millions of them, some healthy, some not so healthy, some costly, some cheap, some easy, some hard. Perhaps the least costly, easiest, and most healthy approach is right here in your hands—writing in a journal!

Journaling is superior to drinking in most ways. It may not go as well as wine with cheese and it may not have the satisfying burn of good Scotch, but with writing there are no calories, no stumbling, no barfing, and few hangovers. You can journal in places where drinking is frowned upon, like at work or in your therapist's waiting room. It's unlikely that a night of journaling will lead to a regrettable phone call to your ex.

The benefits of journaling are as well documented as the benefits of a stiff drink. As noted self-help guru Deepak Chopra claims, "Journaling is one of the most powerful tools we have to transform our lives." According to a widely cited study by James W. Pennebaker and Janel D. Seagal, "Writing about important personal experiences in an emotional way...brings about improvements in mental and physical health." Proven benefits include better stress management, strengthened immune systems, fewer doctor visits, and improvement in chronic illnesses such as asthma.

It's not entirely clear how journaling accomplishes all this. Catharsis is involved, but many also point to the value of organizing experiences into a cohesive narrative. According to *Newsweek*, some experts believe that journaling "forces us to transform the ruminations cluttering our minds into coherent stories." In many ways, journaling enables us to see beyond the present moment to the future we want to create.

Specialists agree that in order to reap the benefits of journaling you have to stick with it, quasi-daily, for as little as five minutes at a time (though at least fifteen minutes is best), even on the worst days. Unlike drinking, journaling every day without fail is actually a good thing. Finding regular writing times and comfortable locations can help with consistency. If you're unable to think of anything to write, don't stress. Instead, use the quotes inside this journal as a jumping-off point for observations and explorations.

Write whatever comes, and don't criticize it; journaling is a means of self-reflection, not a structured composition. Write about the things that are driving you to drink. Rant about your frustrations, your fears, and the things that are making you angry. Write the things you're afraid to say out loud. In other words, spew (so to speak). Finally, determine a home for your journal where you can find it easily, like in the liquor cabinet.

The irritations and tragedies of the world aren't going away. We just have to do what we can to get through the day and enjoy the things that don't suck. So get to journaling and enjoy a drink if that's your pleasure. Just don't drive while doing either. While you're at it, sing a little ditty from J. R. R. Tolkien: "Ho! Ho! Ho! To the bottle and journal I go / To heal my heart and drown my woe."

You look like I need a drink.

David Sedaris

WHY I NEED A DRINK TODAY:

_____

_____

_____

_____

_____

_____

_____

_____

_____

_____

_____

_____

_____

_____

_____

_____

TODAY'S PREFERRED LIQUID ESCAPE:

Three be the things
I shall never attain:
Envy, content, and
sufficient champagne.

Dorothy Parker

WHY I NEED A DRINK TODAY:

_____

_____

_____

_____

_____

_____

_____

_____

_____

_____

_____

_____

_____

_____

_____

_____

TODAY'S PREFERRED LIQUID ESCAPE:

I like to taste it slowly. The first quiet drink of the evening in a quiet bar— that's wonderful.

Raymond Chandler

WHY I NEED A DRINK TODAY:

_____

_____

_____

_____

_____

_____

_____

_____

_____

_____

_____

_____

_____

_____

_____

_____

TODAY'S PREFERRED LIQUID ESCAPE:

Ho! Ho! Ho! to the bottle I go
To heal my heart and drown my woe.

J. R. R. Tolkien

DATE		

WHY I NEED A DRINK TODAY:

_____

_____

_____

_____

_____

_____

_____

_____

_____

_____

_____

_____

_____

_____

_____

_____

TODAY'S PREFERRED LIQUID ESCAPE:

A little nonsense now and then, is relished by the wisest men.

Roald Dahl

WHY I NEED A DRINK TODAY:

_____

_____

_____

_____

_____

_____

_____

_____

_____

_____

_____

_____

_____

_____

_____

TODAY'S PREFERRED LIQUID ESCAPE:

The wine—it made her limbs loose and liquid, made her feel that a hummingbird had taken the place of her heart.

Jodi Picoult

DATE		

WHY I NEED A DRINK TODAY:

_____

_____

_____

_____

_____

_____

_____

_____

_____

_____

_____

_____

_____

_____

_____

_____

TODAY'S PREFERRED LIQUID ESCAPE:

When you drank the world was still out there, but for the moment it didn't have you by the throat.

Charles Bukowski

WHY I NEED A DRINK TODAY:

_____

_____

_____

_____

_____

_____

_____

_____

_____

_____

_____

_____

_____

_____

_____

TODAY'S PREFERRED LIQUID ESCAPE:

There's no app for a bourbon buzz
on a warm day in a cool, dark bar.
The world will always want a drink.

Gillian Flynn

WHY I NEED A DRINK TODAY:

TODAY'S PREFERRED LIQUID ESCAPE:

He was alone with his thoughts. They were extremely unpleasant thoughts and he would rather have had a chaperon.

Douglas Adams

DATE

WHY I NEED A DRINK TODAY:

_____

_____

_____

_____

_____

_____

_____

_____

_____

_____

_____

_____

_____

_____

_____

TODAY'S PREFERRED LIQUID ESCAPE:

I have to start
writing things down.
I also have to start
drinking heavily.

Samantha Jones

WHY I NEED A DRINK TODAY:

TODAY'S PREFERRED LIQUID ESCAPE:

Oh, you hate your job? Oh my God, why didn't you say so? You know, there's a support group for that. It's called *everybody*. They meet at the bar.

Drew Carey

DATE		

WHY I NEED A DRINK TODAY:

_____

_____

_____

_____

_____

_____

_____

_____

_____

_____

_____

_____

_____

_____

_____

_____

_____

TODAY'S PREFERRED LIQUID ESCAPE:

Modern life, too, is often a mechanical oppression and liquor is the only mechanical relief.

Ernest Hemingway

WHY I NEED A DRINK TODAY:

TODAY'S PREFERRED LIQUID ESCAPE:

Turn off your mind,
relax, and float
downstream.

John Lennon

WHY I NEED A DRINK TODAY:

_____

_____

_____

_____

_____

_____

_____

_____

_____

_____

_____

_____

_____

_____

_____

_____

_____

TODAY'S PREFERRED LIQUID ESCAPE:

I like on the table,

when we're speaking,

the light of a bottle

of intelligent wine.

Pablo Neruda

DATE		

WHY I NEED A DRINK TODAY:

_____

_____

_____

_____

_____

_____

_____

_____

_____

_____

_____

_____

_____

_____

_____

_____

_____

TODAY'S PREFERRED LIQUID ESCAPE:

In New York at the end of the day I play ostrich. I take a glass of beer or wine or a pill and go to sleep to have energy for the next day.

Anaïs Nin

DATE

WHY I NEED A DRINK TODAY:

_____

_____

_____

_____

_____

_____

_____

_____

_____

_____

_____

_____

_____

_____

TODAY'S PREFERRED LIQUID ESCAPE:

Think of your head as an unsafe neighborhood; don't go there alone.

Augusten Burroughs

WHY I NEED A DRINK TODAY:

TODAY'S PREFERRED LIQUID ESCAPE:

One sip of this
Will bathe the drooping
spirits in delight,
Beyond the bliss of
dreams.
Be wise, and taste.

John Milton

WHY I NEED A DRINK TODAY:

_____

_____

_____

_____

_____

_____

_____

_____

_____

_____

_____

_____

_____

_____

_____

_____

_____

TODAY'S PREFERRED LIQUID ESCAPE:

There are two kinds of people I don't trust: people who don't drink and people who collect stickers.

Chelsea Handler

WHY I NEED A DRINK TODAY:

_____

_____

_____

_____

_____

_____

_____

_____

_____

_____

_____

_____

_____

_____

_____

_____

TODAY'S PREFERRED LIQUID ESCAPE:

There comes a time
in every woman's life
when the only thing
that helps is a glass
of champagne.

Bette Davis

DATE

WHY I NEED A DRINK TODAY:

_____

_____

_____

_____

_____

_____

_____

_____

_____

_____

_____

_____

_____

_____

_____

TODAY'S PREFERRED LIQUID ESCAPE:

Let's have a party. Let's have it tonight.

Lilly Pulitzer

WHY I NEED A DRINK TODAY:

_____

_____

_____

_____

_____

_____

_____

_____

_____

_____

_____

_____

_____

_____

_____

_____

TODAY'S PREFERRED LIQUID ESCAPE:

There are strings in the human heart which must never be sounded by another, and drinks that I make myself are those strings in mine.

Charles Dickens

WHY I NEED A DRINK TODAY:

TODAY'S PREFERRED LIQUID ESCAPE:

Mendacity is a system that we live in. Liquor is one way out an' death's the other.

Tennessee Williams

WHY I NEED A DRINK TODAY:

_____

_____

_____

_____

_____

_____

_____

_____

_____

_____

_____

_____

_____

_____

_____

_____

TODAY'S PREFERRED LIQUID ESCAPE:

We all want to escape our circumstances, don't we?

Benedict Cumberbatch

WHY I NEED A DRINK TODAY:

_____

_____

_____

_____

_____

_____

_____

_____

_____

_____

_____

_____

_____

_____

_____

TODAY'S PREFERRED LIQUID ESCAPE:

Wine is bottled poetry.

Robert Louis Stevenson

WHY I NEED A DRINK TODAY:

_____

_____

_____

_____

_____

_____

_____

_____

_____

_____

_____

_____

_____

_____

_____

_____

TODAY'S PREFERRED LIQUID ESCAPE:

[She] would have been raucous, unendurable—except through the rosy spectacles of intoxication.

F. Scott Fitzgerald

WHY I NEED A DRINK TODAY:

TODAY'S PREFERRED LIQUID ESCAPE:

The only way of rendering life endurable is to drink as much wine as one can come by.

James Branch Cabell

WHY I NEED A DRINK TODAY:

_____

_____

_____

_____

_____

_____

_____

_____

_____

_____

_____

_____

_____

_____

_____

TODAY'S PREFERRED LIQUID ESCAPE:

You ought to get out of those wet clothes and into a dry martini.

Mae West

DATE

WHY I NEED A DRINK TODAY:

_____

_____

_____

_____

_____

_____

_____

_____

_____

_____

_____

_____

_____

_____

_____

_____

_____

_____

TODAY'S PREFERRED LIQUID ESCAPE:

I do not think stress is a legitimate topic of conversation, in public anyway. No one ever wants to hear how stressed anyone else is, because most of the time *everyone is stressed out.*

Mindy Kaling

WHY I NEED A DRINK TODAY:

_____

_____

_____

_____

_____

_____

_____

_____

_____

_____

_____

_____

_____

_____

_____

TODAY'S PREFERRED LIQUID ESCAPE:

The big winner was alcohol, a lot of alcohol.

Ellen DeGeneres

WHY I NEED A DRINK TODAY:

_____

_____

_____

_____

_____

_____

_____

_____

_____

_____

_____

_____

_____

_____

TODAY'S PREFERRED LIQUID ESCAPE:

Wine; a constant proof that God loves us, and loves to see us happy.

Benjamin Franklin

	DATE	

WHY I NEED A DRINK TODAY:

_____

_____

_____

_____

_____

_____

_____

_____

_____

_____

_____

_____

_____

_____

_____

TODAY'S PREFERRED LIQUID ESCAPE:

After the first glass of absinthe you see things as you wish they were. After the second you see them as they are not. Finally you see things as they really are, and that is the most horrible thing in the world.

Oscar Wilde

	DATE	

WHY I NEED A DRINK TODAY:

_____

_____

_____

_____

_____

_____

_____

_____

_____

_____

_____

_____

_____

_____

TODAY'S PREFERRED LIQUID ESCAPE:

I drink to make other people interesting.

George Jean Nathan

WHY I NEED A DRINK TODAY:

_____

_____

_____

_____

_____

_____

_____

_____

_____

_____

_____

_____

_____

_____

_____

TODAY'S PREFERRED LIQUID ESCAPE:

The best of life is
but intoxication.

Lord Byron

WHY I NEED A DRINK TODAY:

TODAY'S PREFERRED LIQUID ESCAPE:

No live organism can continue for long to exist sanely under conditions of absolute reality.

Shirley Jackson

WHY I NEED A DRINK TODAY:

_____

_____

_____

_____

_____

_____

_____

_____

_____

_____

_____

_____

_____

_____

_____

_____

TODAY'S PREFERRED LIQUID ESCAPE:

How do you feel?
Terrible. I must've
gone to bed sober.

Dashell Hammett

WHY I NEED A DRINK TODAY:

_____

_____

_____

_____

_____

_____

_____

_____

_____

_____

_____

_____

_____

_____

_____

_____

TODAY'S PREFERRED LIQUID ESCAPE:

There's wisdom in wine.

Jack Kerouac

WHY I NEED A DRINK TODAY:

_____

_____

_____

_____

_____

_____

_____

_____

_____

_____

_____

_____

_____

_____

_____

TODAY'S PREFERRED LIQUID ESCAPE:

The only time I ever enjoyed ironing was the day I accidentally got gin in the steam iron.

Phyllis Diller

DATE

WHY I NEED A DRINK TODAY:

_____

_____

_____

_____

_____

_____

_____

_____

_____

_____

_____

_____

_____

_____

_____

_____

TODAY'S PREFERRED LIQUID ESCAPE:

Candy
Is dandy
But liquor
Is quicker.

Ogden Nash

WHY I NEED A DRINK TODAY:

_____

_____

_____

_____

_____

_____

_____

_____

_____

_____

_____

_____

_____

_____

_____

_____

_____

TODAY'S PREFERRED LIQUID ESCAPE:

And if we sip the wine, we find dreams
    coming upon us

Out of the imminent night.

D. H. Lawrence

WHY I NEED A DRINK TODAY:

_____

_____

_____

_____

_____

_____

_____

_____

_____

_____

_____

_____

_____

_____

_____

TODAY'S PREFERRED LIQUID ESCAPE:

Some of us look for the Way in opium and some in God, some of us in whiskey and some in love.

W. Somerset Maugham

	DATE	

WHY I NEED A DRINK TODAY:

_____

_____

_____

_____

_____

_____

_____

_____

_____

_____

_____

_____

_____

_____

_____

TODAY'S PREFERRED LIQUID ESCAPE:

When I
read about
the evils of
drinking,
I gave up
reading.

Henny Youngman

DATE		

WHY I NEED A DRINK TODAY:

_____

_____

_____

_____

_____

_____

_____

_____

_____

_____

_____

_____

_____

_____

_____

_____

_____

TODAY'S PREFERRED LIQUID ESCAPE:

In a new study, scientists are reporting that drinking beer can be good for the liver. I'm sorry, did I say "scientists"? I meant "Irish people."

Tina Fey

	DATE	

WHY I NEED A DRINK TODAY:

_____

_____

_____

_____

_____

_____

_____

_____

_____

_____

_____

_____

_____

_____

_____

_____

_____

TODAY'S PREFERRED LIQUID ESCAPE:

Twenty-four hours in a day, twenty-four beers in a case. Coincidence?

Stephen Wright

DATE		

WHY I NEED A DRINK TODAY:

_____

_____

_____

_____

_____

_____

_____

_____

_____

_____

_____

_____

_____

_____

_____

_____

_____

TODAY'S PREFERRED LIQUID ESCAPE:

The light music of whisky falling into glasses made an agreeable interlude.

James Joyce

DATE		

WHY I NEED A DRINK TODAY:

_____

_____

_____

_____

_____

_____

_____

_____

_____

_____

_____

_____

_____

_____

_____

TODAY'S PREFERRED LIQUID ESCAPE:

Weekend's here, good God almighty,

I'm going to get drunk and be somebody

Toby Keith

WHY I NEED A DRINK TODAY:

_____

_____

_____

_____

_____

_____

_____

_____

_____

_____

_____

_____

_____

_____

_____

_____

TODAY'S PREFERRED LIQUID ESCAPE:

He could
use a
drink. Or
a thousand
of them.

Stephen King

WHY I NEED A DRINK TODAY:

_____

_____

_____

_____

_____

_____

_____

_____

_____

_____

_____

_____

_____

_____

_____

_____

_____

TODAY'S PREFERRED LIQUID ESCAPE:

It's not true that
you shouldn't drink
alone: these can be
the happiest glasses
you ever drain.

Christopher Hitchens

	DATE	

WHY I NEED A DRINK TODAY:

_____

_____

_____

_____

_____

_____

_____

_____

_____

_____

_____

_____

_____

_____

_____

_____

TODAY'S PREFERRED LIQUID ESCAPE:

Ashes to ashes, dust to dust,

If the women don't get you then
  the whiskey must.

Carl Sandburg

DATE

WHY I NEED A DRINK TODAY:

_____

_____

_____

_____

_____

_____

_____

_____

_____

_____

_____

_____

_____

_____

_____

_____

TODAY'S PREFERRED LIQUID ESCAPE:

Give me wine to wash
 me clean
of the weather-stains
 of cares

Ralph Waldo Emerson

WHY I NEED A DRINK TODAY:

_____

_____

_____

_____

_____

_____

_____

_____

_____

_____

_____

_____

_____

_____

_____

TODAY'S PREFERRED LIQUID ESCAPE:

I wasn't capable of being in the world, and I knew that if I tried to go back into it before I was ready, I would be crushed.

Paul Auster

WHY I NEED A DRINK TODAY:

_____

_____

_____

_____

_____

_____

_____

_____

_____

_____

_____

_____

_____

_____

_____

_____

TODAY'S PREFERRED LIQUID ESCAPE:

What can equal a mother's love?
Except a good drink of whisky.
Where's that bottle?

William Faulkner

WHY I NEED A DRINK TODAY:

_____

_____

_____

_____

_____

_____

_____

_____

_____

_____

_____

_____

_____

_____

_____

_____

TODAY'S PREFERRED LIQUID ESCAPE:

Humanity I love you because

when you're hard up you pawn your

intelligence to buy a drink

e. e. cummings

WHY I NEED A DRINK TODAY:

_____

_____

_____

_____

_____

_____

_____

_____

_____

_____

_____

_____

_____

_____

_____

_____

TODAY'S PREFERRED LIQUID ESCAPE:

This river that is the taker-away
   of pain,

And the giver-back of beauty!

Edna St. Vincent Millay

DATE

WHY I NEED A DRINK TODAY:

_____

_____

_____

_____

_____

_____

_____

_____

_____

_____

_____

_____

_____

_____

_____

_____

TODAY'S PREFERRED LIQUID ESCAPE:

What care I how time advances?
I am drinking ale today.

Edgar Allan Poe

WHY I NEED A DRINK TODAY:

_____

_____

_____

_____

_____

_____

_____

_____

_____

_____

_____

_____

_____

_____

_____

_____

TODAY'S PREFERRED LIQUID ESCAPE:

Here at this table, I'm able to leave it behind

Drink till I'm dreamin' a thousand miles out of my mind

Waylon Jennings

WHY I NEED A DRINK TODAY:

_____

_____

_____

_____

_____

_____

_____

_____

_____

_____

_____

_____

_____

_____

_____

_____

TODAY'S PREFERRED LIQUID ESCAPE:

Alcohol tells truth, but its truth is not normal.

Jack London

DATE		

WHY I NEED A DRINK TODAY:

_____

_____

_____

_____

_____

_____

_____

_____

_____

_____

_____

_____

_____

_____

_____

_____

TODAY'S PREFERRED LIQUID ESCAPE:

A good gulp of hot whiskey at bedtime— it's not very scientific, but it helps.

Sir Alexander Fleming

DATE		

WHY I NEED A DRINK TODAY:

_____

_____

_____

_____

_____

_____

_____

_____

_____

_____

_____

_____

_____

_____

_____

_____

_____

TODAY'S PREFERRED LIQUID ESCAPE:

Drink! for you know not whence
  you came nor why:

Drink! for you know not why you
  go, nor where.

Omar Khayyam

WHY I NEED A DRINK TODAY:

_____

_____

_____

_____

_____

_____

_____

_____

_____

_____

_____

_____

_____

_____

_____

_____

TODAY'S PREFERRED LIQUID ESCAPE:

Ale, man, ale's the stuff to drink

For fellows whom it hurts to think.

A. E. Housman

WHY I NEED A DRINK TODAY:

_____

_____

_____

_____

_____

_____

_____

_____

_____

_____

_____

_____

_____

_____

_____

_____

TODAY'S PREFERRED LIQUID ESCAPE:

Any thing for a quiet life: my nose itch'd, and I knew I should drink wine, or kiss a fool.

Jonathan Swift

DATE

WHY I NEED A DRINK TODAY:

_____

_____

_____

_____

_____

_____

_____

_____

_____

_____

_____

_____

_____

_____

_____

_____

_____

TODAY'S PREFERRED LIQUID ESCAPE:

I could not live without Champagne. In victory I deserve it. In defeat I need it.

Winston Churchill

DATE		

WHY I NEED A DRINK TODAY:

_____

_____

_____

_____

_____

_____

_____

_____

_____

_____

_____

_____

_____

_____

_____

TODAY'S PREFERRED LIQUID ESCAPE:

I would kill
everyone in
this room
for a drop
of sweet
beer.

Homer Simpson

DATE

WHY I NEED A DRINK TODAY:

_____

_____

_____

_____

_____

_____

_____

_____

_____

_____

_____

_____

_____

_____

_____

TODAY'S PREFERRED LIQUID ESCAPE:

It pickles my kidneys, yes. But what does it do to my mind? It tosses the sandbags overboard so the balloon can soar. Suddenly I'm above the ordinary. I'm competent.

Billy Wilder

WHY I NEED A DRINK TODAY:

_____

_____

_____

_____

_____

_____

_____

_____

_____

_____

_____

_____

_____

_____

_____

TODAY'S PREFERRED LIQUID ESCAPE:

Whiskey, like a beautiful woman, demands appreciation. You gaze first, then it's time to drink.

Haruki Murakami

WHY I NEED A DRINK TODAY:

_____

_____

_____

_____

_____

_____

_____

_____

_____

_____

_____

_____

_____

_____

_____

_____

_____

TODAY'S PREFERRED LIQUID ESCAPE:

I have to go out every night.
If I stay home one night I start
spreading rumors to my dogs.

Andy Warhol

WHY I NEED A DRINK TODAY:

_____

_____

_____

_____

_____

_____

_____

_____

_____

_____

_____

_____

_____

_____

_____

_____

TODAY'S PREFERRED LIQUID ESCAPE:

Far above him a few white clouds were racing windily after a pale gibbous moon. Drink all morning, they said to him, drink all day. This is life!

Malcolm Lowry

WHY I NEED A DRINK TODAY:

_____

_____

_____

_____

_____

_____

_____

_____

_____

_____

_____

_____

_____

_____

_____

_____

_____

_____

TODAY'S PREFERRED LIQUID ESCAPE:

Pour me somethin' tall an' strong

Make it a Hurricane before I go insane

It's only half-past twelve but I don't care

It's five o'clock somewhere

Alan Jackson

WHY I NEED A DRINK TODAY:

TODAY'S PREFERRED LIQUID ESCAPE:

Without question, the greatest invention in the history of mankind is beer. Oh, I grant you that the wheel was also a fine invention, but the wheel does not go nearly as well with pizza.

Dave Barry

	DATE	

WHY I NEED A DRINK TODAY:

_____

_____

_____

_____

_____

_____

_____

_____

_____

_____

_____

_____

_____

_____

_____

_____

_____

TODAY'S PREFERRED LIQUID ESCAPE:

When I look back on it, all of our important decisions have been figured out when we were drinking.

Raymond Carver

WHY I NEED A DRINK TODAY:

_____

_____

_____

_____

_____

_____

_____

_____

_____

_____

_____

_____

_____

_____

_____

_____

TODAY'S PREFERRED LIQUID ESCAPE:

Hey bartender pour 'em hot tonight

'Til the party and the music and the truth collide

Lady Antebellum

DATE

WHY I NEED A DRINK TODAY:

_____

_____

_____

_____

_____

_____

_____

_____

_____

_____

_____

_____

_____

_____

_____

TODAY'S PREFERRED LIQUID ESCAPE:

It was a maddening image, and the only way to whip it was to hang on until dusk and banish the ghosts with rum.

Hunter S. Thompson

DATE		

WHY I NEED A DRINK TODAY:

_____

_____

_____

_____

_____

_____

_____

_____

_____

_____

_____

_____

_____

_____

_____

TODAY'S PREFERRED LIQUID ESCAPE:

Is there any wine left or did the chicken drink it all?

Don Draper

WHY I NEED A DRINK TODAY:

_____

_____

_____

_____

_____

_____

_____

_____

_____

_____

_____

_____

_____

_____

_____

_____

TODAY'S PREFERRED LIQUID ESCAPE:

Chloroform would be better, or the kick of a mule; but in their absence you must put up with a cocktail.

H. L. Mencken

WHY I NEED A DRINK TODAY:

_____

_____

_____

_____

_____

_____

_____

_____

_____

_____

_____

_____

_____

_____

_____

_____

_____

TODAY'S PREFERRED LIQUID ESCAPE:

Come, gentlemen, I hope we shall drink down all unkindness.

William Shakespeare

WHY I NEED A DRINK TODAY:

_____

_____

_____

_____

_____

_____

_____

_____

_____

_____

_____

_____

_____

_____

_____

_____

TODAY'S PREFERRED LIQUID ESCAPE:

Please don't drive drunk, okay?...But by all means, walk drunk. That looks hilarious.

Amy Poehler

WHY I NEED A DRINK TODAY:

_____

_____

_____

_____

_____

_____

_____

_____

_____

_____

_____

_____

_____

_____

_____

_____

_____

TODAY'S PREFERRED LIQUID ESCAPE:

Yeah, now raise your goblet of rock.
It's a toast to those who rock.

Mike White

DATE

WHY I NEED A DRINK TODAY:

_____

_____

_____

_____

_____

_____

_____

_____

_____

_____

_____

_____

_____

_____

_____

TODAY'S PREFERRED LIQUID ESCAPE:

I'm for anything that gets you through the night, be it prayer, tranquilizers, or a bottle of Jack Daniel's.

Frank Sinatra

WHY I NEED A DRINK TODAY:

TODAY'S PREFERRED LIQUID ESCAPE:

Bottoms up.

Knock Knock

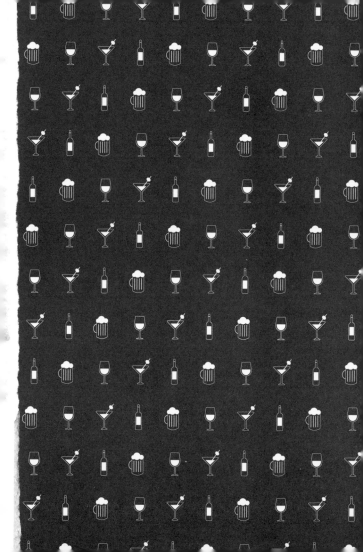

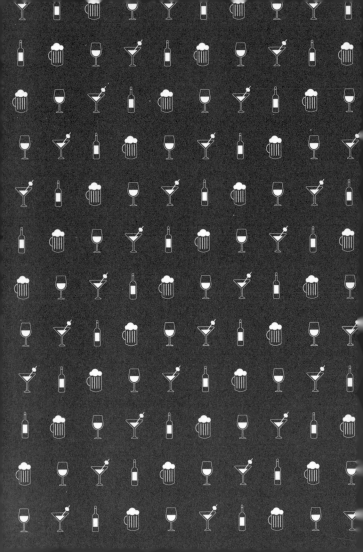